USING THIS BOOK

One of the best ways of helping children read is to read stories to them and with them.

If you have been reading earlier books in this series, you will be used to reading the story from the left-hand pages only, with words and sentences under the illustrations for the children to read.

In this book, the story is printed on both the left- and right-hand pages.

The first time you read the book, read the whole story, both left- and right-hand pages, aloud to the child and look at the illustrations together.

The next time the book is read, you read the text on the left-hand page and the child, in turn, reads the text on the right-hand page, and so on through the book.

© Text and layout SHEILA McCULLAGH MCMLXXXV
© In publication LADYBIRD BOOKS LTD MCMLXXXV
Loughborough, England
LADYBIRD BOOKS, INC.
Lewiston, Maine 04240 U.S.A.

Printed in England

When
the Clock
Struck Thirteen

written by SHEILA McCULLAGH
illustrated by JON DAVIS

This book belongs to:

Ladybird Books

An old house stood in the middle
of a town.
It stood in the middle of a garden.

An old man lived
in the old house.
The old man was a magician.

The house had a strange clock.
The clock was in a little tower,
on the roof of the house.
A bell hung in the tower,
just under the clock.
There was a boy,
who was made of iron,
near the clock.

The iron boy stood
by the bell.

The boy had a silver hammer.
At one o'clock, the iron boy
lifted his silver hammer.
He struck the bell once.
Dong!

At two o'clock, the iron boy
lifted his silver hammer.
He struck the bell twice.
Dong, dong!

At three o'clock, the iron boy
lifted his silver hammer.
He struck the bell three times.
Dong, dong, dong!

At four o'clock, the iron boy
lifted his silver hammer.
He struck the bell four times.
Dong, dong, dong, dong!

And so it went all day
and all night,
every day for many years.
At every hour, the iron boy
struck the bell with his silver hammer.
But one night, everything changed.

The sun had set,
and the moon came out.
The moon shone down
on the old house.
The moon shone on the clock, and
it shone on the iron boy.

The hands of the clock
moved on to twelve.
The iron boy lifted
his silver hammer.

He struck the bell twelve times.
Dong, dong, dong, dong, dong, dong.
Dong, dong, dong, dong, dong, dong!

Midnight!

But then a very strange thing happened.

The iron boy lifted
his silver hammer
and struck the bell again!

17

He had struck the bell thirteen times!
And suddenly, the iron boy found
that he was free.
All his life, his feet
had been fastened to the stones
of the old house.
He had never done anything
but strike the bell.
But now he could move.
At first, he could scarcely believe it.
He lifted one foot.
Then he lifted the other.
It was true! He **could** move!

The iron boy looked down
on the roof of the house.
He saw a skylight in the roof.
The skylight was open.
A light shone in the room below.

The iron boy climbed slowly
down the roof.
He felt very stiff to begin with,
but as he went on, he moved more easily.
He made his way down to the skylight.

He looked down, into the room.
The Magician was sitting by a fire.
He was fast asleep, in his chair.

The iron boy dropped down
into the room below.
He landed on the floor
with a crash.

The Magician woke up.
He saw the iron boy.

"What on earth are **you** doing here?"
cried the Magician.
"You're supposed to be up on the roof,
by the clock. You're supposed to be
striking the bell."
"I've been striking that bell
for years and years,"
said the iron boy.
"I've always struck the right time,
until tonight.
But tonight it was different.
At midnight, I struck the bell
thirteen times—and I was free!"

24

The Magician looked at the iron boy.
"Do you want to be free?" he asked.
"I want to be free,"
said the iron boy.

"Are you sure?" asked the Magician.
"The world is a dangerous place.
You're quite safe, up there
by the clock.
All you have to do
is to strike the bell.
It's a useful thing to do.
Everyone who hears you,
knows what time it is."

"I want to be free,"
said the iron boy.
"I want to be free."

The Magician sighed.

"I want to be free," said the iron boy,
"and what is more, I want to grow up.
I want to be alive.
I've seen children alive in the lane,
as I've stood up there by the clock.
I want to be like them."

The Magician sighed again.

"I have a magic silver dust,
that makes toy animals come alive,"
he said. "But it doesn't work
with people. It will be very difficult
for you to change into a real boy."

"I don't care," said the iron boy.
"I want to be alive."

The Magician sighed once more.
He picked up an old map
that was lying on the table.

"You will have to go away,"
said the Magician.
"You will have to go
a long way away."

"I will go anywhere,"
said the iron boy.
"Then you must go on a long journey,"
said the Magician.
"A long way away,
there is a magical country.
It is the Country of Zorn."
He unrolled the map.
"You must go to the Country of Zorn,"
he said. "And when you get there,
you must find your way
to the Blue Mountains.
High up in the Blue Mountains
you will find the Silver River.
The river runs down the mountain,
and into a great cave.
If you bathe in the Silver River,
you will become really alive."

"How can I get there?"
asked the iron boy.
"How can I find the way?"

The Magician got up, and
put away his map.
"I can send you to the edge of the
Country of Zorn in a flying saucer,"
he said. "But after that,
you must find your own way
to the mountains.
It will be a dangerous journey.
You would be much safer,
if you stayed here with me."

"When can I go?"
asked the iron boy.

"You can start at once,"
said the Magician.
"I will send you off
in the flying saucer."
"I'm ready," said the iron boy.
"But before I go,
please tell me my name."
"You don't have a name," said the
Magician.
"You will find a name,
when you bathe in the Silver River."

There was a big saucer
on the table.

The Magician picked up the iron boy,
and put him down in the middle
of the saucer.

"You're quite sure that you want to go?"
he asked.

"If you go to the Country of Zorn,
you can never come back."

"I'm quite sure," said the iron boy.

"I want to be alive."

"Very well," said the Magician.
"I will let you go.
The flying saucer will take you there,
and fly back here to me."

The Magician muttered a spell.
He put his hand on the flying saucer,
and pressed a red button.
Then he snapped his fingers.

The saucer flew up off the table.
It flew to the window.
The window blew open.
The flying saucer flew
out the window.

The moon was shining down.
The flying saucer flew over the roofs
of the town. It flew over the houses
and over the trees,
over the hills and under the stars.
It flew to the edge of the Country of
Zorn, carrying the iron boy.
The flying saucer landed
in the Country of Zorn,
and the iron boy stepped out.
He was standing at the edge
of a forest.
The iron boy looked
at the dark trees. A big white owl
came flying over the treetops,
and...
But that is another story.

The iron boy in the Country of Zorn

Notes for the parent/teacher

In the books in Stage 4, the child is asked to read part of the story and not just the sentences under the illustrations. This is a big step forward.

If you read the whole story to the child first, it will make the reading much easier for her.* But some children still need the chance to read quietly to themselves the pages that they will later read aloud with you.

Reading a story aloud on sight, without having had a chance to look at the text first, is one of the most advanced and difficult kinds of reading. When the child is reading aloud, if she reads the words in such a way that the story makes sense but the words are not exactly the same as those in the book, don't correct her on the first reading. If she does it the next time you read the book together, you might ask the child to look a little more carefully. For example, if on page 13, the child reads "The sun had gone down," instead of "The sun had set," let it pass on the first reading. This kind of mistake shows that the child understands the meaning of the printed text, even though she gives that meaning in

---

* In order to avoid the continual "he or she," "him or her," the child is referred to in this book as "she." However, the stories are equally appropriate for boys and girls.

her own words and not the words in the book. Even skilled readers do this sometimes. On later readings, ask the child to look carefully at what is there in the book.

If a child is stuck at a word, you can simply say what the word is. There are three other useful ways of helping a child discover what the word might be:

(a) *looking at the illustration for clues;*

(b) *reading the sentence again from the beginning after the child has looked at the picture;*

(c) *skipping the word the child doesn't know and reading on to the end of the sentence.*

If she still can't "guess" the word, or if she shows any sign of becoming worried, tell her what the word is.

*Remember always that both you and your child should **enjoy** your reading sessions. Figuring out a word she doesn't know should be almost a game from the child's point of view. Approach words in this way yourself, helping the child to look for "clues."*

Keep the book even when the child can read her part of it easily and has gone on to other, more difficult books. Children will later reach a stage when they can read the whole story for themselves.

The story in this book ends when the iron boy arrives in the Country of Zorn.

*All these books are in **Stage 4**.*

2 **The Sandalwood Girl**
is the story of what happens to a girl carved out of wood, who was in the attic of the old house when the clock struck thirteen.

The story of the iron boy continues in
3 **On the Way to the Blue Mountains**
which tells about the adventures of the iron boy and the sandalwood girl as they go on their dangerous journey.

4 **The Fire in the Grass**
continues their adventures.

5 **The Silver River**
tells how the children are carried to the Blue Mountains by silver ponies. When the boy and girl have bathed in the river, they become ordinary children and finally meet someone who tells them their names.

More suggestions for helping children read the books in this series will be found in the *Parent/Teacher Guide*.